THE BEATLES:
Yesterday...Today...Tomorrow

Rochelle Larkin

2A

SCHOLASTIC BOOK SERVICES
New York Toronto London Auckland Sydney Tokyo

1st printing . . . . May 1974

Printed in the U. S. A.

Table of Contents

YESTERDAY

"Yesterday
All my troubles seemed so far away..."

John.
Paul.
George.
Ringo.

    Four faces that became as familiar as our own.
Four names that meant more to more people than
any others in the world. "For ever," was chanted in
the streets, "Beatles for ever!" That was the
password we used in those days, but it wasn't to turn
out anything like that.

    They had started playing together in 1962,
although they had been playing with each other and
others before that. They had hit the top in England in
1963. They stormed and conquered America in 1964.
They were the undisputed kings not only of music,
but of all pop culture, with every new album and
every new attitude being even more influential than
the one before it. They could do almost no wrong.
Then, in 1970, it was all over. The greatest
supergroup the world had ever known broke up.

All endings must have beginnings, and to find out why the four-part Beatles' harmony came to a discordant end, we must go back to their yesterday.

The Beatles, a rock group made up of four young men — John Lennon, Paul McCartney, George Harrison, and a drummer named Pete Best — had attracted a large following among young fans in their home town of Liverpool. Their popularity extended throughout England, and as far away as Hamburg, Germany, a music-mad city where they had played several grueling "gigs." Requests for one of their little-known recordings by a customer brought them to the attention of a young businessman, Brian Epstein. Brian thought they had great potential and arranged record auditions for them in London. He agreed with John, Paul, and George that their drummer was not of the same musical caliber as the

The Beatles — Paul McCartney, George Harrison, John Lennon, and Ringo Starr — as we first knew them. Original publicity photos, sent out just prior to the first American visit.

three of them were, and that although Pete had a great following among the fans, he simply wasn't good enough to record. The three boys wanted to give the spot to a friend of theirs who played drums for a rival group on the Liverpool-Hamburg circuit. The friend was Richard Starkey. Starkey always wore at least four or five rings on his fingers, and had been aptly nicknamed Ringo. Starkey was shortened, to reflect his aspirations in life, and thus was born Ringo Starr.

The Beatles were now set. There were loud outcries from Pete Best's loyal fans. Though the three boys hated to do it, they knew they had to weather this storm for the future of the group; they had worked too hard not to give it everything they could. They felt they were on the brink of success.

The Beatles at a rehearsal with movie star Marlene Dietrich for their first Command Performance before British royalty. It was at this show that John told the audience, "Those in the cheaper seats, clap. The rest of you, rattle your jewelry," a remark repeated around the world. UPI

Facing the controversy over the firing of Pete Best was undoubtedly a good move. In addition to furthering the performing needs of the group, it gave all four first-hand experience in facing controversies, of which there would be so many in the wake of the world-wide fame that was so soon to come to them.

While the four forever-Beatles were facing their audiences in Liverpool and touring England, they were also anxiously waiting for news to break on their first British-produced record, "Love Me Do," backed with "P.S. I Love You." Although Liverpool was already immersed in the first wave of Beatlemania, they were not well-known outside their home town. Touring helped somewhat, but the Beatles knew, as did manager Brian Epstein and everyone else in the business, that the only way for any musical act of any kind to make it big was through records.

Records and radio airplay of the records were the key ingredients to success. It was true not only in England, but in the United States, Europe, and the rest of the world. A few hundred people saw you at a concert, maybe a few thousand if you played some really large arena, but if you cut a hit record, it would be bought and listened to by millions of people everywhere. In an age of instant mass communications, the record was the performers' medium. Records were big business, and the royalties from the sale of discs and radio airplay were the performers' principal source of income. This is still true.

Recording, of course, means even more to the conscientious artist. In the studio there is almost complete control of the performance; whatever doesn't sound right can be corrected immediately and re-recorded. There is no way to create onstage the effects that the Beatles were later to put into their music. It would be impossible to mount "Sgt. Pepper" properly on any stage in the world. But of course, all that was far ahead of the Beatles. What they needed now was the hit that would bring them recognition. They knew they were good; it was for the rest of the world to find it out.

Of that the Beatles had no doubt whatsoever. All the work they had done over the past few years told them so. The horrible working conditions in Hamburg, where they played for ten or twelve hours a day, seven days a week, months at a time, had tightened them up in a way nothing else could have. They lived in terrible cramped quarters and there was little relaxation or diversion except for their music. They could read each other perfectly, and Ringo, who had often sat in with them in Liverpool and Hamburg, before actually joining the group, was so familiar with their sound he had no trouble fitting right in. John and Paul had started writing their own songs, which they much preferred, even though onstage they still did a lot of other people's material.

At last, the famous four arrive on our shores. The first trip in February, 1964 was made primarily for television appearances on the Ed Sullivan Show and they visited only New York, Washington, and Miami. UPI

"Love Me Do" started getting airplay, but it never went higher than seventeenth on the British charts. The Beatles kept on touring. Their record producer, George Martin, had found another song he wanted them to do for their second release, but they didn't want to record it. John and Paul had written "Please Please Me" and that was the tune they wanted to do next. Their insistence on having their way does a lot to demonstrate how the Beatles thought of themselves. They were still an unknown struggling group from provincial Liverpool. Even better-known artists usually gave in to the dictates of their producers, who were, after all, connected with the record companies and used to calling the turns. But the Beatles persisted, and since even Martin thought it was a terrific tune, the Beatles finally won.

"Please Please Me" was recorded in November 1962, but not released until the following January. Between those two dates, the boys played their last Hamburg engagement, appeared at their old haunt, the Cavern in Liverpool, and were the number-two or -three attraction on several tours.

One month after being released, "Please Please Me" became the number-one record in England. Slowly the phenomenon that had started in Liverpool and was to become known throughout the world as Beatlemania began to spread through the British Isles. Fans, especially girls, would start lining up days in advance to buy tickets for their scheduled appearances. Special police guards had to be called out to hold back the crowds when they did appear. Screaming hysteria began to drown out their performances. Soon the Beatles were a group you went to see; hearing them was impossible. Suddenly, there were riot conditions everywhere they appeared. Then the jelly-bean thing started. George

6

Another first: a silver disc for "Please Please Me," the first Beatle song to hit number one. After it, there was no stopping until they had received more awards for record sales than anyone else in history.

had mentioned in an interview that he liked jelly beans. Soon they were being pelted with the hard little things at every performance. The long hairstyle they had picked up in Europe became known as the Beatle haircut and began appearing on young men all over England. The revolution had begun.

All this adulation was to have a startling effect on the lives of four boys, still in their early twenties, who came from working-class families and who had had to do all sorts of dull jobs before fame descended on them. Even after "Please Please Me" was released, there was still some question in their families as to whether they'd ever be able to earn their living this way. Their parents saw the music business as full of uncertainty, with no guarantees, no security, and maybe no future. Even after Brian had become their manager and was trying to make a record deal for them, they still held down their dull, dead-end jobs that represented real security to their families. The only person ever to have as much faith in them as they had in themselves was Brian Epstein.

The Beatles had dickered with Epstein for several months after their first meeting before they would sign a contract with him. But when they did, they knew it was the most important step they had ever taken in their lives. They still had to go to Germany, they still had to fill other dates that had been arranged before Brian had started making the rounds of record companies. When things got really terrible, in Hamburg or on the road in England, or when the pressures from their families became overwhelming, they could continue because there was someone pleading their cause. There was someone providing the spark of hope that they would indeed some day make it big.

Of course, Brian provided them with much more than psychological support. Until he took over, the Beatles had been very casual about their onstage attitudes and business responsibilities. It was Brian who forbid them to eat or drink while publicly performing. Unbelievable as it seems now, that was actually their practice. It was a holdover from Hamburg, where the nightclub managers hadn't given them time off for meals. And in the rough-and-ready atmosphere of the Liverpool clubs, there was very little formality. The boys thought nothing of downing a couple of Cokes and hamburgers between tunes. Brian thought very little of it too! He ordered an immediate end to such unshow-businesslike habits, and the boys meekly obeyed. Their rather proper manager also did not care too keenly about the way they dressed. The early Beatles' garb was a style that was a combination of the Elvis Presley image and the British teddy boys. The teddy boys were young delinquents of the fifties who affected a very tough pose. From them, the Beatles took the idea of lots of black leather, unshaven faces, and a generally rough untidy look. From Elvis they borrowed those old standbys of the American West, cowboy boots and jeans. Brian cleaned the closets. In came matching uniforms of suits, dress shirts, and ties. They were to look polished and professionally successful, even if they weren't.

Brian was right, of course. By making the Beatles conform outwardly, they gained respect and the right not to conform in other ways.

At first the Beatles, especially John, rebelled against the new look. He felt they weren't being their true selves. But he went along, and as the uniforms took on more and more individuality, they too began to be copied by other groups and fans. As with the long hair, the uniforms, dubbed "mod," set a new style all over the world. And when the Beatles finally stopped wearing them, the Edwardian collars, shaped waists, and bell-bottomed trousers had already left an indelible mark on male fashions. When the foursome opted for more freedom in their clothing, with influences ranging from Nehru Indian to American Indian, men's wear underwent the greatest revolution since the loincloth.

Beatlemania was now in full swing. The third record, "From Me to You," quickly rose to number one, and with the fourth release, "She Loves You" with its yeh-yeh-yeh refrain, the explosion was worldwide. It was the fall of 1963 and there was no longer any question of whether they were going to make it. If there was any question at all, it was instead, "How long could it last?"

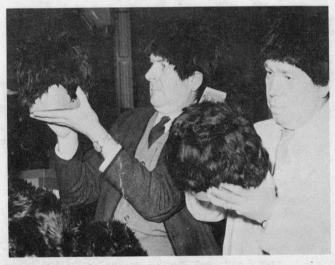

At the height of Beatlemania, there was scarcely an item imaginable that wasn't available with the Beatle imprint, including synthetic wigs to give the Beatle look to a still short-haired world. UPI

According to fans who greeted them in New York early the following year, the answer was "Beatles forever." The British Isles, which had made them number one for so many months now, could no longer contain them. Their first trip to the United States, while not a nationwide tour, was their greatest triumph yet. All America, it seemed, wanted to see the moptops who had turned the usually conservative, staid old mother country topsy-turvy. The British newspapers and the international wire services had made the Beatles famous before they even got here, and the America, which had been so saddened recently by the assassination of its young President, was more than ready to receive these four new heroes.

First on the bandwagon were the disc jockeys, who bombarded their listeners with Beatle news and Beatle music for weeks before the foursome arrived. They vied with each other to provide the audience with the most Beatle sounds, hoping to win more listeners for their stations. They staged contests and recorded interviews were broadcast that made it sound as if the boys were talking personally to the D.J. By the time the plane landed that fateful February afternoon, the whole country seemed near hysteria.

But more conservative elements were quick to pull in the opposite direction. Teachers, ministers, politicians began to make dire predictions about the group, whose influence on the young they knew would be strong. Rock and roll was denounced, as it always had been by these spokesmen, even more vehemently than before since it could be directed against a specific target.

When the four targets landed, most of the fire went out of the cannons. Here were four boys even

11

mothers could love. True, there was more hair on their heads than they were used to seeing on boys, but such angelic faces peered out from beneath the bangs. And who could object to the innocence of lyrics like, "I Want to Hold Your Hand"? After a decade of the writhing and wriggling of Elvis and the other heavy rockers, the clean demeanor of the Beatles looked positively heaven-sent. Brian Epstein had indeed been right. The moms of America proved it.

The country went wild. The boys made two appearances on the Ed Sullivan television show and it was estimated that the audience that tuned in those Sunday nights was the largest in history. They played sell-out concerts in New York, Washington, and Miami Beach. It was as if everything had been magnified ten times. There were no arenas in England that could hold the enormous crowds that

The first American television appearance. The Beatles are in rehearsal clothes as technicians make their final checks.
UPI

showed up, clamoring for tickets for each American concert. At home, two thousand fans was a riot-size crowd. In Washington, twenty thousand showed up. And not only were the kids crowding in, but business jumped on the bandwagon too. Brian was bombarded by as many offers as the Beatles themselves, although of a completely different nature.

Manufacturers were among the first to spot the trend. The public that was breaking down doors at record stores would want everything that was labeled "Beatles." That meant: tee shirts, wigs, dolls, clothes hangers, posters, books, toys, linens, buttons, pillows, and anything else you could think of.

"Everytime they spell beetles with an 'a' we make money," John chortled. And they surely did, for themselves and for everyone connected with them. A Beatles-starring movie was even projected.

Every success breeds imitation and the Beatles were no exception. But groups such as this were short-lived. (There was even an oriental group that called itself the Japanese Beatles!) UPI

Tired but triumphant, the Beatles went home to plan this new phase of their lives and to cope with the incredible problems that this incredible success had brought. While the cocky quartet had always predicted success for themselves, no one, not even the brilliant Brian Epstein, could have dreamed that it would be this enormous. It became impossible for them to lead anything that even approximated a normal life.

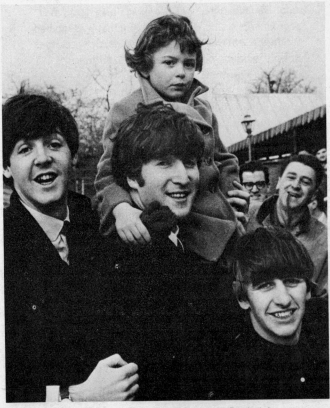

A playful moment during that first hectic visit. Paul, John, and Ringo entertain a young fan in New York's Central Park on one of the few occasions they saw anything besides hotels, theaters, and studios. UPI

Local fans camped out in front of their modest family homes and when they bought newer, larger houses for their parents, the fans followed them to the new locations. George's mother, who could never turn people away, especially those she felt were responsible for her son's popularity, would serve tea and cookies to all who came. All the parents were modest people who did not want their lives made "uppity" by their sons' success. They wanted to stay in their old neighborhoods among the friends and family they had always known. Ringo's parents were the last holdouts. But staying in Liverpool had become impossible. Even the tourists, who had never made the city one of the musts on a trip to England, now came in hordes to see where the Beatles had lived, worked, and gone to school. The Cavern, where they had played almost three hundred times, became a Beatles shrine.

*The first concert in New York City's Carnegie Hall. Seats had to be placed onstage to accommodate the overflow. The crowd outside filled the streets and jammed traffic for blocks. Police were onstage as well as in front. Fans were never to get this close ever again. And the Beatles could be **heard!** UPI*

It sounds fabulous, but it wasn't. For John, who had married his school sweetheart, Cynthia, it became a nightmare. They had a little boy, Julian (named for John's mother, Julia, who had been killed by a car when John was in his teens). It was impossible for Cynthia to take the baby for a walk. Ever since they had been married, she had had to deny being Mrs. Lennon, but now it was worse. They feared for the baby's safety. Not that anyone would wish him harm, but as Ringo put it, when his wife Maureen gave birth to their son Zak, "Some fan might just decide to take him for a souvenir!"

Both the Lennons and the Starrs bought homes near each other in a secluded, exclusive suburb, a private development in Weybridge, Surrey. George married a model named Pattie Boyd, whom he had met on the first day of filming their first movie, *A Hard Day's Night*. They bought a house in another secluded English suburb. And when Paul, after several headline romances, finally married an American heiress, Linda Eastman, they settled down on a large farm in Scotland, in the distant Argyllshire region. (Except for the Scottish retreat, all the other houses have since been found out and given up.)

John and Paul manage an afternoon of sea and sun during the Miami Beach stopover where they taped their next television appearance. UPI

Plans had been made for a second trip to the United States even before their first visit was over. But on this second trip the Beatles would see even less of America than America would see of them. The country became a swiftly-passing montage of hotel and motel rooms, frenzied fans, leaps into limousines and, when the limousines failed to provide adequate protection, helicopters, used to hasten them to and from concert dates.

The frenzy attendant on this first full American tour in August of 1964 could never be adequately captured on paper. (The Beatles were coming off their biggest times ever.) Two months before, in June, they had started touring again, first in Europe, where crowds of as many as 100,000 people showed up at airports to see them. In Australia the reports were that there were 300,000 in Adelaide. In July, English royalty attended the opening of *A Hard Day's Night*, which was acclaimed by critics everywhere as one of the freshest, funniest films in many years. The Beatles' brand of comedy was compared favorably with that of the Marx Brothers.

The American tour lasted from August 19 to September 20. It covered twenty-four cities — if you count New York twice — and started in San Francisco. The Beatles dominated the news. Newspapers and airwaves were full of nothing but the Beatles. Their every word was seized on, reported, repeated, and analyzed, as older America, while not quite disapproving of them (who could?), failed to understand why they attracted millions of young followers in a way no one else had. Adults could dig the music, buy the records, and proudly proclaim themselves Beatles fanciers but they never did get to the core underneath all the publicity and hysteria. But so overwhelming was the influence of the Beatles on all aspects of pop life and style throughout the sixties, that there was nothing to do but accept it and keep trying to understand. What most of the critics and other adults never realized was that they were trying to analyze feeling rather than thinking. Emotional responses such as the Beatles aroused do not lend themselves to analysis; it's like trying to define the word love.

In England, the largest theaters held 2,000 people. Now, the audience was 20,000 and still growing. At this concert, a revolving stage was provided so everyone could see the new idols of the world.

Back in the British Isles, the boys do a film about themselves. It was becoming economically unsound to tour in
the small English theaters and filming was a way of letting
the fans see them. UPI

As the Beatles' artistry increased, so did the interest of other artists in them. Here a London sculptor exhibits his interpretation of the foursome. It sold for $4,500. UPI

A candid moment during a recording session. The famous moptops are starting to get a little longer as the Beatles lead the way to even more extreme styles for men.

And love is really what it was all about! The whole world was having a love affair with the Beatles. But for the four objects of all that affection life was anything but romantic. The mass hysteria created a need for security measures that even the most fanatic potentate never dreamed of. The boys were like the eye of a raging hurricane. Everything whirled around them, but they had to be encapsulated and protected from it all. Whatever spare time they had was spent among themselves, their road manager, Neil Aspinall, and their general do-all, Mal Evans. The latter had been the burly bouncer at Liverpool's Cavern. Part of the jobs of these two was to make sure the Beatles were fed. Such food as they got had to be brought to their rooms, and rather than dining in the style that would have been more appropriate to their sudden wealth, dinner usually consisted of a few grabbed hamburgers washed down with Cokes.

Ringo gives the okay sign as he leaves a London Hospital after an attack of tonsilitis. He was in for eight days and away from singing for an additional two weeks, a bleak stretch of 1964 for his enormous army of fans. UPI

Theoretically, they were already millionaires, but their life style while on tour in the richest country in the world wasn't much different than that of those grubby old days in Hamburg! One big difference, however, was the amount of time they spent onstage. In Hamburg, the sets had lasted for hours. The last concert in the United States, a charity performance in the famous old Paramount Theater in Times Square, lasted a bare twenty minutes! And although they were making piles of money, it never had any reality to them. If they made ten thousand dollars a night or a hundred thousand, they had to do the same amount of work and go through the same changes. They seldom saw any actual cash. In fact, they usually just carried pocket money. Brian made the deals and the only thing the Beatles saw were contracts, not cash, a situation Paul put to very good use a few years later when he wrote, "You never give me your money/ You only give me your funny paper." Balance sheets and bank notes and other financial records didn't mean very much to boys who had spent their lives having to watch every penny, who had lived in a world where hard cash spoke in the loudest voice and anything else scarcely above a whisper. Now they knew they were rich, but it didn't have any concrete meaning. Not while they were touring, and all the money in the world couldn't protect them from the fans or soften conditions on the road.

Once they got back to England, it was different. Nobody had to worry about down payments or mortgages when they started to buy all those houses for themselves and their families! There was more than enough money for any material things they would ever want or need. They could go into the recording studio, as they did a few years later, and have whole huge orchestras and special effects that cost more money than anyone had ever spent recording before. But there was no money that could stave off the rigors of the road.

They're back! The Beatles say hello to England after capturing those outposts of the empire, Australia and New Zealand. To the country "down under" goes the honor of bringing out the greatest number of fans ever to greet the Beatles, 100,000 at the airport in Adelaide. UPI

In America, it was the fatiguing zigzagging in jets from one part of the country to another. Back in little England, it was much different and in some ways far worse. There, even after the fantastic success of the American tour, they still traveled from city to city in a car, driving all night, through snow or storms, to reach the site of the next concert. For some reason, the American tours were made during the summer and the British tours in winter. And the British climate, far from the best in the world, is especially bad in winter. Once more they were pent up in hotels, guarded by police, being toted sandwiches and such by Neil and Mal. They had little relaxation and few diversions. The tours had become endless, mindless, funless affairs. They were, of necessity, as isolated from their fans and the rest of humanity as they had been flying over America in their jets and helicopters. It is probably more than coincidental that Ringo got married shortly after the first extended American tour and that George did the same after the enormous tour of 1965.

HIGHLIGHTS OF THE GREAT AMERICAN TOUR,
SUMMER 1964

The Beatles hold a press conference in Los Angeles be-
fore the start of their 23-city tour. UPI

On stage at the Cow Palace, San Francisco. In this picture, you can almost hear them singing. But the audience couldn't — they were screaming too loud! UPI

They played to an overcapacity crowd in Las Vegas, the town that thought it had seen everything in entertainers before! UPI

Another outdoor sports park. There were few indoor auditoriums that were big enough for the crowds. That's why American tours were done in warm weather. UPI

Back in New York for the Forest Hills concerts, they were greeted by fans who had camped at the airport for days. UPI

The Beatles touch down in Toronto for their first Canadian concert. Ringo was in the next limo. UPI

They leave for home in September, exhausted but exhilarated by the unbelievable response from their fans. UPI

The fact that they couldn't be heard during their concert appearances was getting to them too. Before, it had all been a big joke, but there was now a big difference. The Beatles suddenly wanted very much to be heard.

They were writing a different kind of song by the end of 1965. Gone were the simpleminded lyrics about wanting to hold your hand and seeing you standing there, themes that devolved around dances and other teen-age occupations. An entirely new depth and feeling was being sounded in songs like "Day Tripper" and "Paperback Writer." The Beatles, the adolescent phenomenon of all time, had entered the adult world, and the problems and preoccupations of that world suddenly took over the songs. The Beatles had done something no other popular entertainers ever did before — they outgrew many of the fans with whom they had grown up. And the legions of kids now needed someone else to scream about and at, and denounced the Beatles for having joined that other world, the adult world that now discovered the Beatles were witty, sophisticated, intellectually acceptable, and altogether with it. Suddenly all the fun went out and something else took over the boys, the sound, and the clamor. Beatle appreciation became an adult game.

Of course, there were millions of fans who never deserted. College campuses became beehives of Beatle lovers. Young teens who had become young adults in the mid-sixties found that the Beatles were right in there with them as they climbed through their new world. The new Beatles were as satisfying to the new needs as they had been to the old. The big difference for fans at this level was that the music was no longer being denounced by their parents and teachers. They were all tumbling over each other to express their new-found approval of the ex-teen-age idols!

Beatles had become an established, accepted fact of life. Their influence was infinite.

Some of the antics that the Beatles pulled during the making of their first full-length movie were as funny as the stunts that actually appeared in the film. Here Paul hangs overhead for a better view of the proceedings; the crew below were searching frantically for him! UPI

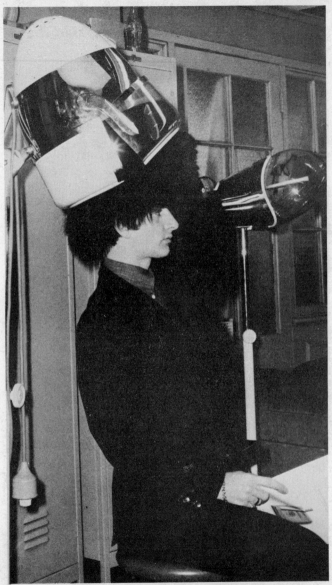

Ringo relaxes with a magazine as his hair is being dried during a break in the filming. UPI

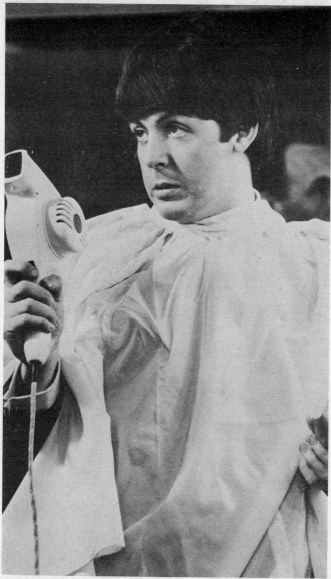

After spying Ringo's "beauty" ritual, Paul decides to take the job in hand instead! UPI

Behind the beard, experimenting with still another hairy style, is John. UPI

Ringo tries his hand at directing the others. There is no record of how well he succeeded. UPI

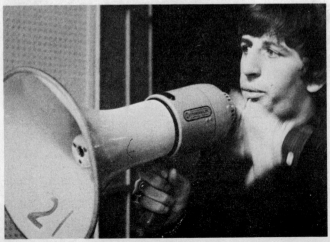

George tries his hand, or rather his foot, at toe dancing.
He met his wife-to-be on the set. UPI

The oversized clothes are supposed to be a disguise for
Ringo, but those rings are a dead giveaway! UPI

Before, the Beatles had played down to their fans somewhat. Kids wanted to hear sweet, simple songs that told of love and romance and were, above all, good to dance to. This the foursome gave them as no other group or single entertainer ever had. But they never tried to stretch the mind of the audience or to use the music as their own means of self-expression. Performing was enough of an outlet for them. But now, with the release of "Rubber Soul" and "Revolver," the writing of the songs became all-important, and performing, especially in the recording studio, became the way to get the message of the songs across. At the same time instrumentalization was becoming as important as the lyrics. Now the Beatles were spending lots of that hard-earned money — on hundreds of additional musicians, on complicated pieces of electronic equipment, on the most advanced features of music-making in the world.

We can use just one song of this period — "Eleanor Rigby" — as an example of all the changes converging at this point:

No pop group had ever used classical musicians, like the section of violinists heard in the background of "Eleanor Rigby." Even if they had, it wouldn't have been possible to include them in a tour for the sole purpose of playing this one particular song.

Yet if "Eleanor Rigby" were performed shorn of all the accoutrements, how could the Beatles sing it to an audience of screaming fans who wouldn't even be able to hear it? And threw jelly beans to boot?

No one ever dances to "Eleanor Rigby," yet it is one of the most important songs written in this century. It would take a four-hundred-page book to express what the Beatles put together in three short verses — the loneliness and isolation of people now, and the helplessness of religion to provide the comfort it did in earlier times. Now this is a profound set of ideas, much more likely to appear in weighty volumes than in a popular song. Yet "Eleanor Rigby" remains also one of the *loveliest* of all Beatle compositions, still being sung and recorded by as wide a range of singers as any song ever written by anyone. It is the perfect example of what the Beatles in the very time of their greatest success and popularity set out to do, and, once again, did better than anyone else ever had.

It was an accomplishment that the whole world acclaimed. To the Beatles, however, it was the final nailhead driven into the coffin of touring. Backed with "Yellow Submarine," another turning point to be discussed later on, "Eleanor Rigby" was released as a single in August 1966. The last appearance of the Beatles onstage together as a group was on August 29, 1966, in San Francisco. It was the last performance of the four and the last American tour. Last, last, last, at last, was the way they themselves felt about it.

What would be next? Well, the very first thing the Beatles had to contend with was the growing number of rumors that they were breaking up. They had given up touring to be able to continue to grow together as a group, to explore all the possibilities they felt that

36

Against a Beatle backdrop, Princess Margaret greets the boys at the premiere. She was the guest of honor. UPI

A now-familiar scene: the Beatles waving good-bye at London Airport to the fans who never stopped coming to see them off. Note lengthening hair. UPI

they, as the Beatles, were capable of. The marvelous
new songs, the extended time they spent perfecting
each and every track of their albums should have
been proof of that. They tried to reassure the public
that they were still very much together and intended
to remain so.

In Eskimo costume for their London Christmas show, 1964.
UPI

The foursome fooling with bikes in the Bahamas where they went to film the new movie, ''Help!'' UPI

Ringo, recently married, listens to a message from a shell. UPI

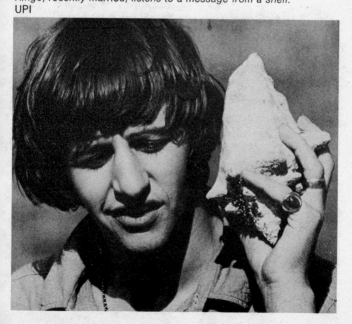

Now that the formalities of touring were over, there was a little time — the first in years for the Beatles — to stretch out as four separate people. George, who had developed an interest in India, and especially its music, while making their second film, *Help!*, took his blonde Patti off on a long trip to that vast exotic country. The results of this trip were to be an influence on the Beatles and their music, indeed, all of popular music, for many years. Meanwhile, the so-called "quiet" Beatle was on his own for the first time since his teens.

John, still in love with making movies, took a part in a film called *How I Won the War*. He did some traveling and bought a house near Ringo and George for his wife and son. John had written two books, *In His Own Write* and *A Spaniard in the Works*, which had been very well received, in spite of the fact that they had been published at the height of Beatlemania, when anything that any of the Beatles did was looked down on by "serious" people as a publicity gimmick or money-grabber. But no one could deny the cleverness and freshness of those two books, the sharpness of the humor and observation. Even today, they make ticklish reading for anyone who wants to battle his way through John's puns and off-beat comedy of made-up words and in-jokes. Now, with time and money at his disposal, John knew that there were many things he could get into and he began looking around.

Ringo, the real homebody of the group, took special delight in his growing family. He also took parts in two movies, *Candy*, and *The Magic Christian*, and for his low-key, appealing portrayals, got much praise. His special essence seems to register well on film. He had in fact in the second Beatle flick, *Help!*, what amounts to the starring role. His little-boy-lost quality delighted directors and audiences alike. But movie-making was of small import to Ringo. Like John and Paul, he had known what it was to grow up in a poor and broken home. Now he was able to provide his family with all the security and luxury anyone could want. This gave him a happiness that the never-never world of fame and success never could. Ringo, more than any of the others, stayed home and *enjoyed* his prosperity.

Part of "Help!" was filmed in Austria and this time wives Cynthia Lennon and Maureen Starr were allowed along. Fans line London Airport to see the group off. UPI

By the year's end, Ringo was a daddy as well. He proudly holds his new son, Zak, a name the fans hated but other Beatles loved. UPI

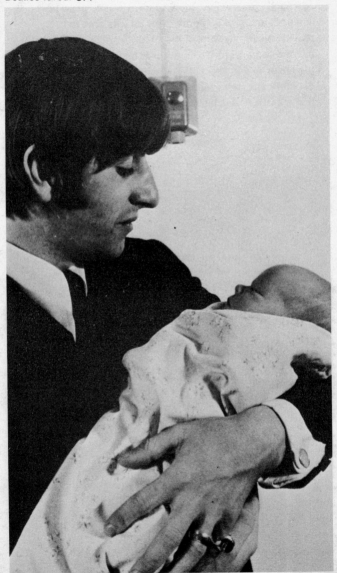

John, in disguise with glasses, manages to escape fans' notice as he and his wife leave England for a trip to film festival in the south of France. UPI

Paul was still the only unmarried Beatle. He had a long-lasting romance with a beautiful girl named Jane Asher, but Jane was an actress with a career of her own to take care of. That meant she could be tied up in a movie or off to the United States, or whatever, in much the same way Paul had been. They never settled permanently, although when she was on the scene Jane was as much a part of the inner circle of Beatle people as any of the wives, Cynthia, Maureen, and Patti. Paul wrote the music for a movie, *The Family Way*, which didn't cause much excitement. He had a house in London, the only Beatle living within the city. This was at the height of the era when the staid old city had been dubbed "Swinging London," an image the Beatles and their music had helped to establish. It was the time of the total British music take-over that the Beatles had spearheaded; the time of the discotheques where thousands of young people flocked nightly to hear and dance to the newest sounds; the time of the boutiques, those strange little stores that cropped up to sell the clothes and accessories that the disco dancers would be parading in; the time of the drugs that were the final element in the new psychedelic whirl of the clothes and the music and the dances. And there was Paul, certainly the handsomest and most romantic of the Beatles, alone and unoccupied in the midst of it. There was no real pressure on him, but perhaps that was the problem. For years now he had lived in total occupation, performing, composing, more involved with Brian Epstein in the business end of it than any of the others. Now he too had time and money, but no family of his own to lavish it on. He took proper care of his father, as did all the Beatles of their parents, but there were no wife and babies to care for. The baby-faced boy who had sung

The Beatles express the same astonishment as the rest of the world when it's announced they have received the highest order of the British Empire, an honor usually reserved for generals and such. Many disgruntled conservatives thought it was the end of the world. In a way, it was — the end of their world and the start of the youth takeover. UPI

Paul, Ringo and his wife, and John with his wife, arrive at the opening of ''Help!'' at the London Pavillion in July, 1965. An ambulance and 250 policemen stood by, just in case. UPI

"Yesterday" so sweetly on television, with the softest of strings in the background, had turned on every female in the world. Yet here he was, at loose ends, alone in a society that cared for nothing except its own pleasure. And as much as Paul tried to fit in with that life of leisure and luxury, there was too much strength in his working-class background and upbringing, too much discipline imposed from the years of Hamburg and Liverpool and touring, not to rebel at the whole thing. Paul needed a way out, and the way he took was drugs.

The Beatles had had some experience with drugs; those eight-hour sets in Hamburg had introduced them to pep pills. Sometime during their touring they had been given pot and had come to depend on it as a relaxant from their abnormal pressures. But Paul went into heavier stuff than that even, and the results were disastrous. He was picked up on a London sidewalk by a policeman early one morning, sitting on someone's stoop, asleep.

Of course, the news made headlines all over the world, and it seemed to bring all the others running to help their mate. They had all been pursuing their separate activities but now once again they centered in London, the scene of their recording triumphs and the arena that had given them overnight recognition.

One of their constant and least demonstrative fans, Princess Margaret attended this opening, too. Here she greets old pal Paul. By that time you had to be a princess in order to get that close to the Beatles. UPI

That had been the night they had played a Royal command performance that had marked the turning point from being merely the sensation of Liverpool to becoming the idols of all England. The three homes were in the suburbs, not far from the town, and once again the foursome were together.

Their last three albums had been tremendous hits — *Rubber Soul, Yesterday — and Today,* and *Revolver* — so there had been no rush to bring out a new one. That was one of the reasons they had been able to go their separate ways for a time. Indeed, fan reaction to the marvelous work they had produced on *Revolver* had even raised the question of whether they would be able to do anything that would top such gems as "Taxman," "Eleanor Rigby," "Good Day, Sunshine," and "Here, There and Everywhere." Even those critics who had admired them from the beginning and applauded loudly at every advance the Beatles had made quietly wondered if they hadn't passed their peak and were in fact already on the way out.

Nothing much was heard from or about them for several months, except rumors that they were in the recording studio spending uncounted sums on a supersecret project. Some people wondered if it were even true that they hadn't disbanded. *Revolver* had been released in August of 1966; now it was already the spring of the next year and there had never been this long a wait between albums before. Then, in June 1967, the Beatles did what the Beatles always did: sprung a surprise on the world of such impact nobody could quite believe it.

And here are the rest of the 55,000! UPI

The name of the surprise was *Sgt. Pepper's Lonely Hearts Club Band*, and with it the Beatles once more turned the world of music upside down. Not only had they surpassed everything they had ever done, they left every other group far behind. There was no more speculation on who the new supergroup would be. The new supergroup would be the same as the old supergroup, only better than ever!

The Beatles had produced an album that was unlike any done before. Prior to *Sgt. Pepper*, every record album was just a collection of songs. *Sgt. Pepper* changed all that. It was promptly dubbed a concept album, meaning that every song was part of the same theme, or concept, of the album, tying in with all the other tracks to produce one unified whole. If it didn't exactly tell a complete story, word for word, it at least illuminated an idea with each song that was part of the same plot. In this case, it was an old-timey band, of the sort that Americans aren't familiar with, but which have been popular in England since the last century. The Beatles wove this brand new idea into some very old materials, including the English music hall type of songs they are so fond of and the centuries-old music of India that George had gotten so caught up in. In the words of the songs, however, they proved once again they understood better than anyone else around what young people had on their minds. And weaving in and out of the many social problems that they explore is an undeniable preoccupation with drugs that alarmed many people. Once again, the Beatles had taken material from their own lives, things that were happening to them — sitar lessons, Paul's drug experiments — and used it to make music that was meaningful to everyone.

Here they show off the controversial medals awarded to them by the Queen of England. John later gave his to his aunt. UPI

Three down, one to go! Gorgeous George takes a bride, model Pattie Boyd. The twosome were married in London on January 21, 1966 and went off for the standard short secret Beatle honeymoon. UPI

"When I'm Sixty-Four" explored, in a lovely way, the anxiety that young lovers feel when they try to imagine the future; the music is exactly the rinky-tinky sort that delights English people of the older generation, so now they too had their own Beatles anthem. "She's Leaving Home" was, like "Eleanor Rigby" before it, an entire novel done in the short space of a song. It voiced the bewilderment of the middle generation, the parents who cannot understand why their daughter won't accept the values and standards that rule their lives. "A Day in the Life" expressed the alienation with the perplexing world of today that affects every age group. And even in the midst of all this problem-facing the Beatles must prove they haven't lost that famous touch of humor and here they do it with the bouncy, funsy, "Lovely Rita," their ode to the ladies who check the parking meters. Quite a range of subject matter to be presented in one record album, even by this famous foursome!

Japanese Beatles for real? They arrive in Tokyo in June, 1966 in the standard gear of the country at the start of a long tour through the Orient. UPI

Even the busy, garish cover of the album tells you that the Beatles are ready to take on the whole world. Although the boys themselves, in appropriately Sgt. Pepper-y outfits, dominate the center, they have surrounded themselves with people from their own, and everyone else's past. The four themselves, in a photo from the earlier shirt, suit, and tie stage are there, along with movie stars from silent films up to the present, famous historical figures from the wax museum, personal idols Bob Dylan and Muhammad ali, whom they had met on their first American trip, and Indian idols set among the flowers that decorate what could easily be a Beatle grave.

"Sgt. Peppers Lonely Hearts Club Band" has just been released and the Beatles gather to receive both the acclaim and acknowledge the controversy after one of the tracks had been banned by British radio. UPI

Some controversy was raised over the songs that were held to be drug-connected. "A Little Help From My Friends" talked about getting high. The initials in the name "Lucy in the Sky with Diamonds" were said to stand for LSD. Although John has insisted that the phrase is one that his little boy brought home from school, to describe a drawing he had made of a little girl schoolmate, the lyrics of the song, full of psychedelic images, can certainly be interpreted in many ways. But since the Beatles were quick to deny both the drug message and drugs themselves very soon after the release of the album, the controversy spun itself out and most every track on the album came to be a contemporary classic. Paul admitted using LSD but denied that it had value.

That the songs are extraordinary is beyond question. "With a little help from my friends" has become part of the general vocabulary. The number of different versions of all the songs on the album done by other singers runs into the hundreds. It may not seem like such an unusual idea any more, because so many other concept albums appeared in the wake of this one. For a time, every singer worth his salt had to come out with a concept album. Most of them are long forgotten, but if not for *Sgt. Pepper* there might never have been a *Tommy* or a *Jesus Christ Superstar*. They are but extensions of the idea first developed by the Beatles in this great breakthrough album.

Again, the four were the foremost in the pop music world. They went back to work almost at once on another concept.

This time it was an even larger concept. They would produce an album, yes, but not just an album this time. Paul wanted to do a film, a film they would completely control by themselves. They wanted it not

Meeting the press on their last tour, August, 1966. John was explaining his remark about the Beatles being more popular than Christ. He said he was merely referring to the decline in church attendance. UPI

After the Beatles announced they would no longer tour, the rumor mills began working overtime on speculation that the group was breaking up. The Beatles, who were working on their most complex recordings ever, faced the press and denied all the stories. UPI

for theaters, but to show in England on television on the day after Christmas, which is traditionally a big family holiday, and then hopefully, to the rest of the world. Paul's idea was that since they had essentially been playing themselves in their films, they might as well do a film about themselves. They were into mysticism by this time, the middle of 1967, having heard about the religions and philosophies of the East from George and his wife. Pattie had already joined an Indian religious group on her own earlier in the year. They would hire a bus, load it with their friends and head for an unknown destination, accompanied by all the technicians necessary for making a movie. The bus would roll, the cameras would roll, and thus would be produced the *Magical Mystery Tour*. Besides, it would all be a lot of fun. It would prove the Beatles could take anything, give it the magic touch of their personalities and turn it into gold.

The whole affair ended up proving that the Beatles were human after all and could make mistakes just like everybody else. It was a unmitigated disaster.

Since it was more or less Paul's idea, he was producer, director, and film editor, none of which functions he knew anything about. The film was shown on British television where it was most unappreciated. Plans for showing it elsewhere were quickly withdrawn.

The failure of the film was linked to another tragic event. Barely had they started filming it when Brian Epstein was found dead. The coroner's final report ruled it due to an accidental overdose of sleeping pills. The Beatles and everyone connected with them were shaken up.

Brian had been a successful but obscure businessman when he first met them. His family

owned a small string of furniture stores in the
Liverpool area and after trying his hand at several
things that didn't work out, he joined the family
business, managing the music departments in the
stores.

*Displaying a model of the famous craft which, along with
"Sgt. Pepper" inspired the story line of the full-length car-
toon. Four new songs, as well as some of their best earlier
tunes, would be included in the soundtrack. UPI*

Here he seemed to have found himself. The most important item under his supervision was records, and Brian worked out a system whereby he would never be out of stock. He prided himself on the fact that a customer could come into the store and get any disc asked for; if it was something new, he would have it in a matter of days.

But when two or three customers came in asking for a record by the Beatles, Brian was stumped. None of his suppliers had ever heard of the group. The record itself, he found out, had been made in Germany. The persistence of the fans intrigued him, and when he was told that the Beatles were a local group, who played at the Cavern most frequently, Brian did something he had never done before: He went to the basement club to hear them. While this may not sound so strange to us now, you have to remember that Brian was a quiet young man from a conservative family and the Cavern was the gathering place for the wildest young fans to hear the wildest new music. The club ran day and night, playing lunchtime sets that were very popular with the girls working in the area. By this time, the Beatles were so adored in Liverpool that girls would arrive at the club with their hair in rollers, and make a mad dash to the ladies' room just as the group preceding the Beatles would be finishing. This way they could really look fresh and cool on the one-in-a-million chance that one of the foursome might spot them! (Ringo actually met his wife Maureen at the club. She had been a hairdresser then, so maybe she knew something that the other girls didn't!) It was strictly a rough, working-class crowd, not at all Brian's sort of scene. But something drew him there as if it had been ordained, and subsequently, to millions of fans, it sort of was.

His first reaction to the group was mixed: As unfamiliar as it was to him, he liked their music. Even more so, he was impressed by the fanatical reaction of the audience. What he didn't like about the·Beatles was their messy appearance, their jeans and leather jackets, their unprofessional habit of eating onstage. But instinctively he knew they were something out of the ordinary. And just as surely he knew a whole new phase of his rather uninteresting, unsuccessful life was about to start.

The Beatles try on some Pepper-ish costumes as they pose for artists on the long-in-production animated film, "Yellow Submarine."

He had several meetings with the Beatles. He was unsure in his own mind what he wanted to do with them, but he was becoming more and more bored with his work at the store. Finally, he offered them a plan: He would manage them, try to get recording work for them, build them into the kind of top act that their talent warranted, and promote them all over England and perhaps to even more distant horizons. In exchange, he wanted obedience: He would pick their clothes, set their image, conduct all their business. He agreed that he would never interfere with the music, openly admitting that he knew nothing whatever about the Beatle sound except that he liked it and thought the rest of the world could grow to love it.

After not too much haggling, the four then-Beatles agreed. Pete Best was still on drums at that time, and Brian's biggest job at first was getting all four of them to all their gigs on time. There was no engagement accepted unless Brian first approved the terms of the contract, and once he did, it was as binding as the Bible. He deplored the haphazard manner in which they had conducted themselves, sometimes showing up for a job, sometimes not, as the mood hit them. He put an end to that with his strict discipline. The boys resented it, but were shrewd enough to know that Brian's way was the only way to make things work.

Brian himself worked like crazy for them. He traveled up and down the country, shouting their praises, getting them better bookings for more money than they had ever made. He turned them from another scruffy-looking big-beat group into charming professionals. He knocked on the doors of all the record companies in England, trying to get them auditioned. He plied the entertainment writers with stories about his great group, trying to get them some publicity. And as if this wasn't enough headache for someone who wasn't experienced in those phases of the business, John, Paul, and George soon handed him his most difficult assignment of all — they wanted Pete replaced before they had any recording auditions lined up. They were convinced they needed a better drummer, and that that drummer was Ringo Starr.

For someone who wasn't very good at handling people, Brian had a tough job. Pete had not only shared the roughest of the rough times with the boys, his mother had been enormously helpful in giving them work at her own club when they were down and out. They had used her house to rehearse in for hours on end. And now Pete had to be told not only that he was out, just as they were on the verge of success after all the tough times, but that he was out because he wasn't good enough. Brian didn't like doing it, but he had promised that he would never interfere with the music, and since he was the manager he had to do it.

If Pete was bitter, the fans were outraged. In Liverpool, he was as popular as any of the other three, and those rough-tough girls in the rollers went berserk. They carried signs reading "Pete Forever, Ringo Never" and they meant it. But the Beatles stood their ground, and Ringo prevailed. Brian worried a lot, but they came through the crisis knowing that they were a team. Now, Brian felt, they were really ready to record. He made the arrangements with George Martin that led to the release of "Love Me Do" and that was when his own career as manager went into high gear.

The next several years with the Beatles provided all the challenge and excitement a man could ever

John and wife at the opening of "How I Won the War," his first non-Beatle movie. UPI

expect from his career. Although he was given a great deal of the credit for the Beatles' success, he never claimed to have "made" the group as many other managers have. He knew that the Beatles had that certain something special going for them; what Brian did was to harness all that energy, give it direction, and tell the world about it. The Beatles would have been the Beatles without Brian Epstein, but we might never have known about them.

Now they were the superstars of the world, and Brian had an army of helpers to handle what had once been his sole concern. The tremendous amount of work that had gone into setting up the great tours was now a thing of the past. Individually, the four boys had shown they could function on their own without the backup of the rest of the group. Brian was more than ever the fifth wheel on the applecart. He managed a few other Liverpool-based talents, but except for an isolated single hit here or there, none of them ever amounted to much, especially compared to his first and most important clients. Little by little, they either dropped out of the business or went elsewhere for guidance. Brian never had enough time for anyone but the Beatles.

It might have seemed at this point in his life that they didn't have enough time for him, suddenly. A new leader, a new kind of leader, had appeared in their lives, an improbable man with the improbable name of Maharishi Mahesh Yogi. He was, and is, an Indian mystic and philosopher, with an original yet comfortable theory about life that was very suitable for four young millionaires, especially four such as ours, with their interest already whetted by Indian music and fashions. Their minds were totally taken by the Maharishi as they made plans to visit him in India for a long stay. Their financial affairs were run by accountants and attorneys. Their music was developing brilliantly and according to their own desires. What need had the Beatles for Brian Epstein anymore?

Many people close to him think that this kind of reasoning was depressing Brian to the point of his taking pills to push them from his mind. He was basically a loner, with no really strong emotional ties to anyone, while the Beatles always had each other. At this stage of their lives, they often claimed they felt more like four parts of one person than like four separate people. Since their social backgrounds were so similar, they could laugh at the same jokes and inside references that others wouldn't get. Brian wasn't privy to all this; although he was a native of the same town, he had led a different kind of life. His loneliness in the midst of worldwide attention must have seemed especially crushing. Whatever the reason or reasons behind Brian's death, it was something that shattered the Beatles' hard-won complacency. Even at the top of the world, it seemed, life had a way of handing you shocks and problems. The Beatles had never voiced any adverse criticism of Brian's management and they seemed to be genuinely fond of him. They were prevented from showing their grief along with the others who mourned him, as his family was afraid that the appearance of the famous four would trample the dignity of their sorrow. Later, a private service was held for them.

The shock waves of Brian's death had two immediate effects. The month-long trip to meditate with the Maharishi on his home grounds was postponed, as was the work on *Magical Mystery Tour*. The Beatles had to face a sudden new reality — they were millionaires without a manager. All the business problems they entrusted to Brian would have to be dealt with. And it was far from being the situation they were in before Brian. Now they were big business, not a scruffy little group working for a few pounds and shillings. Beatledom was a worldwide empire. A brother of Brian's named Clive started picking up the pieces of Nems, the organization Brian had founded to coordinate his affairs, and on the surface things went along as usual. But the Beatles weren't quite certain that this was how it should be. The matter stayed in the back of their minds.

Ringo in the movie, "The Magic Christian." UPI

The foursome, just before taking the trip to India. "Lady Madonna," had just been released. UPI

In February, Paul, Jane, Maureen, and Ringo fly to India to join George, John, and their wives to study with their new guru, Maharishi Mahesh Yogi, in the Himalaya Mountains.
UPI

Meanwhile, there were all the other things they wanted to do. They had to finish *Magical Mystery Tour*, and they were very involved with the Maharishi. Because of his teachings, the Beatles had become anti-drugs. The death of Brian, diagnosed as from a sleeping pill overdose, drove the point home with finality.

Paul leaves the car as curious Indians look on. UPI

The *Magical Mystery Tour* was finally completed, with the results already described. But if the film was a failure, the album produced from it was not. It includes such songs as "Strawberry Fields" and "Penny Lane," which are among the Beatles' prettiest, and "The Fool on the Hill," considered one of their greatest. "All You Need Is Love," which had been performed by the boys live on television a few months prior, and had become something of an anthem since *Yellow Submarine* used it so extensively, was also included. So is "I Am the Walrus," which created such a stir with its near-nonsense lyrics that fans all over the world tried to interpret with equally nonsensical results. The song really brought the activity of Beatle-interpretation to a new depth. Everyone was sure that Lennon and McCartney were the poets of our age, and some followers persisted in trying to find hidden meanings in every tune. Even when the boys themselves insisted that it was silly to look for something that wasn't there in the first place, the analysts continued. (In their later work, especially their separate efforts, a lot of the obscurity is replaced with simpler, more down-to-earth phrases that speak very clearly for themselves.)

The Beatles spent much more time producing the film than they did producing the songs for it, but it is the songs that will remain and last forever, proving at least two important things. First, people, even Beatles, should do what they know how to do. Second, even Beatles are only people, and as such, can and do make mistakes. The *Magical Mystery Tour* was their first public failure since they hit the top. The film flopped, and the boys flew — to India. The long visit to the Maharishi inaugurated 1968 for them.

Paul with road manager Mal Evans, who went everywhere with the Beatles. They are on the outskirts of the Maharishi's retreat. UPI

Crossing the bridge from the outside world to the otherworldly domain of the mystic. UPI

*John on his way to meditation. The Beatles later left the
Maharishi and discarded most of his teachings.* UPI

Even though it had ended on two bad notes — Brian's death and the *Magical Mystery* mess — the year now tucked behind them was one of unparalleled results. They had produced *Sgt. Pepper*, which alone would have insured them immortality. They had turned their backs on drugs, and were widening the scope of their minds, exploring religion and philosophy with an intentness not ordinarily associated with four barely educated young men.

The Beatles tackled the long and winding roads of Eastern thought with all the vigor at their disposal.

While they did not entirely share the rigors of the other disciples when they got to India, their accommodations were not plush. They did try to travel in privacy, but that was almost entirely an impossibility. Although they themselves did not wish it, there were cameras and reporters on every step of the trip. The Beatles refused to hold press conferences or do anything that would be seen as exploiting their new-found religion. They really went to India to try to get away from the world as much as they could. But try as they might, they did not find the answers in India or in the Maharishi. His theme, Transcendental Meditation, was soon after discarded by them — like another set of clothes that didn't suit them any more. They left his tutelage with misgiving, with more questions raised than answered.

Back to London they went, their two gurus gone. They didn't look for a third. Instead, they looked to themselves. Just prior to going to India, they had released another song, one of their biggest, "Lady Madonna," and songwriting again became upper-most in their minds. The question was, in everyone else's mind at least, what would they do or *could* they do, to top *Sgt. Pepper*?

If music was uppermost, then business was other-most in their thoughts. They decided to do it all themselves. John and Paul flew to New York and held a press conference, their first in ages, to announce the formation of the Beatles' own company, Apple. Why Apple? they were asked, and Paul answered because it was simple — like, A is for Apple in a child's book. But it didn't quite work out that way. Their plans for Apple were too ambitious. They wanted a company not only for their own activities, but for other performers as well. Apple would give money to artists — performers, painters, anybody talented — money that no one else would give them to support their pet projects. The sole approval would come from the Beatles themselves or their appointees. Apple would produce movies as well as records, run shops as well as theaters. It would be big business, all right, but run primarily for the people, the people who deserved and needed support, and it would be run with Beatle money. The Beatles, having made theirs, were now willing to share the profits with their people. All you had to do was ask.

In a happier moment, John and Yoko take his son Julian to a rehearsal of a Rolling Stones show. UPI

If it sounds naive, it was. As with the *Magical Mystery Tour*, the Beatles were stepping out to do something big, armed with nothing but their personalities. They opened a boutique, called Apple, and in a few months were so disgusted with the results they gave everything away free. They found out quickly that whatever they were, they certainly weren't shopkeepers. Unfortunately, neither were the people they hired to run the shop.

One of the Beatles' non-recording ventures, the boutique called Apple, closed for business in a near-riot as clothes were given away. UPI

They opened a big building to house all the various divisions and activities of the new company and of course that location soon became the focal point of all Beatle-watching as well. It became a hangout for all their friends, followers, and fans, who tried by every means possible to gain entry. They had good reason to try. The Beatles were there almost constantly for weeks at a time. They were working on a new album, the real *Sgt. Pepper* follow-up and a new song that wasn't to be included in the album, but released prior to it as a single. The song took almost as much work as the entire album that was to follow it. They hadn't released anything at all since "Lady Madonna" early in the year and now it was late summer. But this one was more than just another single, and they knew it. This one small disc was to shake up the world of the 45 rpm as thoroughly as *Sgt. Pepper* and that of the album. Finally, in September, it was done.

It was called "Hey Jude." It was seven minutes long.

The music business went wild. Ever since the advent of the 45, singles had run about three minutes, a few seconds more or less. Every pop radio station in the United States was geared to this time element. Even the individual tracks on albums adhered to the three-minute length — if its performers and producers wanted airplay, which of course they did. The three-minute record allowed the station to program its hours exactly — so much for music, so much for commercials and other announcements, and so on. A seven-minute record could create havoc with all of that. But so could a station's failure to play the long-awaited new Beatle release. And the stations were well aware of that!

So the playing of "Hey Jude" became an event of sorts on radio stations all over the country. It was announced in advance that it was going to be played at such and such time, and fans dropped everything they were doing in order to listen.

"Hey Jude" is an utterly marvelous song that would have become a hit even if the Beatles had only produced the shorter version that some stations were playing. But all the furor and special announcements didn't hurt a bit. It was a most auspicious beginning, artistically and commercially, for the infant company.

True to their promise, the Beatles did record other performers on the Apple label. One of the happiest of these occurrences was an album by Billy Preston, the soul singer and piano player who had been very popular in the fifties. He had played on some of their own records, and the Beatles loved him. It was the restart of a career that saw the multi-talented American hit the top all over again. They also recorded the English group Badfinger with great results.

As for their own new album, the Beatles surpassed their greatest efforts in quantity, if not always in quality. As if to completely throw away the ornate effects of their earlier presentations (or perhaps to save money, now that they were paying all the bills), the new album was a stark simple white, with nothing, not even a name on it. They didn't waste time trying to think up a tricky title either. It was called *The Beatles,* a name they had never used before on a record. It was, in its simplicity, a good-looking package, and the contents were amply rewarding for any Beatle-lover. First of all, there were thirty songs, almost enough for three albums by anybody else. If not all the offerings were as brilliant and beautiful as *every* track in *Pepper*, some of them were, and many were delightful. Taken all in all, the songs reflect every trend in popular music in the western world of this century. There are of course echoes of the English music hall they always enjoyed using, but there's everything else as well, early and middle Hollywood, wild West, twenties and thirties roo-doo-dee-oh-do, sentimental love songs and a few lyrics that might have raised eyebrows a few years before. You name it, it's there. The album was full of backward glances but it also looked ahead, as

The Beatles, as they appear on "Hey Jude."

the Beatles never failed to do. They had become outspoken in their politics, and "Revolution" did just that — made mention of Chairman Mao as no one would have dared at that time. Even now, with the ice supposedly broken between the Western nations and the East, Chinese Communism isn't exactly material for pop songs. Even the pandas didn't rate that, or the Ping-Pong players. But when the Beatles had no one but themselves to answer to, the results could be fresh and marvelous. *The Beatles* is a wellspring to which musicians and singers would return for many years to refresh themselves.

There was another great project that came to fruition soon after. Except for a small bit at the very end, the Beatles did not appear in *Yellow Submarine*. Even their speaking voices are dubbed by actors imitating them. But the film is Beatles all the way, and as such, it too made a minor revolution.

The Beatles love comics and cartoons and not since the early days of Walt Disney in the thirties had those popular forms been raised to such artistry. People who wouldn't have been caught dead sneaking a peek at most cartoons queued up for hours to see *Yellow Submarine*. You could buy clothes hangers of the animated versions of the foursome, books, magazines, posters, records, toys (including a model of the famous craft itself), and every other item imaginable featuring the funny, wild, and dazzling artwork of the film. The boys were featured as themselves, more or less, and as Sgt. Pepper's Lonely Hearts Club Band. Included in the film, although not on the album, were "Eleanor Rigby," "Nowhere Man," and other gems. The film had great appeal for all ages and once more the Beatles were riding high in public esteem. Privately, it was another matter.

Personal scandal hits John as he and Yoko Ono, the Japanese-born artist, leave a court hearing. He soon filed for divorce from his first wife. UPI

The last Beatle takes the plunge. Paul McCartney marries American Linda Eastman on March 12, 1969 in London. As the Beatles matured, so did the fans and there was little public outcry at this event. UPI

The fading months of 1968 and the cold months of the new year were to see the first Beatle divorce, the last Beatle marriage, and the first Beatle remarriage. The first rumblings came as John started to appear in public with one of the artists who had been attracted to Apple. Her name was Yoko Ono and she was a Japanese-born, American-educated film maker and artist who was well-known in the more avant-garde London circles. She had a child from a prior marriage and was a few years older than John. The gossip reached scandal proportions when John announced that he was leaving his wife and that he and Yoko would marry. They went through several escapades together that made headlines all over the world. Yoko was much criticized for her rather way-out, bohemian appearance. She did not fit the sleek image of the Beatle wives. The fans couldn't believe it. Yoko was an announced feminist too, before women's lib became an acceptable issue, and her art was as unconventional as her appearance. Although she was primarily a film maker and painter, John started recording with her and a group he dubbed the Plastic Ono Band.

In the midst of all the furor over John and Yoko, on March 12, 1969, the last Beatle bachelor, Paul, unexpectedly married an American girl, Linda Eastman. She too, had been married before and had a child. In addition, she was one of the heirs to the vast Eastman Kodak fortune and was very wealthy in her own right. After all the publicity that had accompanied every move of the most sought-after Beatle of all, the marriage came as a big surprise to many people.

If marriage in a registry right in the heart of London was an easy matter for Paul, it was anything but for John and Yoko. There were problems of

Eight days later, John and Yoko cleared all their legal hur-
dles and were able to get married on the island of Gibraltar. This Honeymoon was not to a secret hideaway as all
the others had been but was a well-publicized tour that
included press conferences like this one in Amsterdam.
UPI

citizenship and custody, of pending court hearings for a variety of things that the two had become involved in, and it became increasingly apparent, with much of the world watching, that they would not be able to get married in England at all. After much distress, they were finally able to get permission to wed on the island of Gibraltar, just eight days after the McCartney-Eastman nuptials.

Once more, the Beatles had been reduced to the level of human beings. They had problems in their marriages, just as ordinary people did, they were hassled when they got into trouble, they weren't perfect. But they could do what most ordinary people couldn't — they could take their troubles and turn them into gold by singing about them. "The Ballad of John and Yoko" was John's musical description of their odyssey. Backed with "Old Brown Shoe," it was released in June after their marriage, and it sold over a million records — a solid gold single.

The Beatles came back to London — Paul and Linda from an extended honeymoon of great secrecy, John and Yoko from a headlined honeymoon that included press conferences from Europe to North America, held, said John, in the cause of world peace. They began working on a new album, titled in honor of the street where they recorded it. The cover would show them crossing the same thoroughfare, all in ordinary clothes, except for John's white suit. All had hair longer than shoulder length; Paul was barefoot. It was the first full album in a year, aside from *Yellow Submarine*. The Beatles were back together, but something was different. There had been a change and it would never be quite the same again. They had been separated by their work before. By this time they had each produced separate music, except for Ringo, and he had been off making movies. It was another kind of difference. It was personal. It was the wives.

Paul had not approved of Yoko and he hadn't hidden his feelings from John. It seemed to have blown over, but then got worse after Paul married. John never forgave his buddy for the slights Paul had given Yoko, probably at the time when Paul never thought it was going to be serious between them. Then there were other, subtler pressures. The original wives, Cynthia, Maureen, and Pattie, and the long-steady Jane Asher, were more compliant girls who understood that sometimes their men were Beatles before they were husbands, that the four had something special in their beings as Beatles that was more important than wives. But the new wives were different.

George, with sitar master Ravi Shankar, announces the concert to aid the refugees of Bangladesh. Ringo, Bob Dylan, and other top stars joined to make the event a milestone in modern music. UPI

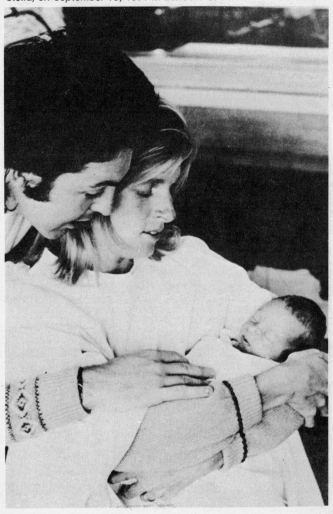

The McCartneys celebrate the birth of their daughter, Stella, on September 13, 1971 in London. UPI

On October 19, 1971, John and Yoko observe his 31st birthday. They were in the city of Syracuse where Yoko's first solo art show was being held. UPI

Yoko had a career of her own. She had an identity independent from that of a Beatle wife. John seemed to be utterly devoted to her and never away from her. He even kept her next to him at recording sessions. Linda was used to independence too, since she was wealthy and was a career photographer of the rock scene. How these two women got along has never been made public. But the elements were all there for discord, and the pressures and problems were mounting.

None of this showed up in their work, although the Beatles often reflected elements of their lives in their music. The album was *Abbey Road*, and it turned out to be as fine as anything they had ever done. It contains shining examples of every facet of their talent. It has songs that are funny, romantic, social. It looks back to early childhood with "Golden Slumbers" and complains about the world of big business in "You Never Give Me Your Money." It teases the Queen and pokes fun at plain people. Perhaps more than any other album, it expresses the Beatles' feeling for nature and its wonders. (A New York television station played "Here Comes the Sun" after showing a total eclipse the next year!) It also proved that George could now compose music that would stand with the best of Lennon and McCartney. "Something" was the song of the year in terms of number of times recorded and played. The year that had started with so many problems ended on a sweet high note of another fine accomplishment, and with plans for more projects in 1970.

There would first be another album, one that would incorporate ten million-selling singles that had never been included on a long-play record before. The tunes ran almost the length of the Beatles' career up to that time, from "Can't Buy Me Love," of early 1964 vintage, through "Paperback Writer" of 1966, through the "Ballad of John and Yoko" of 1969. Since all of the songs had been previously recorded, the Beatles didn't have to do much more for this one than show up to pose for the picture on the cover. The album in honor of its longest track was called *Hey Jude*. If they had ever had it in the back of their minds to produce an album that would be retrospective of all of their work or a crash course in Instant Beatles, this would have done nicely.

George appears on a television talk show to discuss the then upcoming Concert for Bangladesh, an enormous personal triumph for the former "silent" Beatle, and the source of thousands of dollars for the unfortunates whose cause he espoused. UPI

Meanwhile, back at the Apple empire, things were not going so well. Except for the records produced, the original plan was not working out. As businessmen, the Beatles were proving themselves to be somewhat less than superstars. The extravagant headquarters on London's Sevile Row had turned out to be little more than a gathering place for a lot of drifters and hangers-on. A new American manager was brought in as financial advisor and to sort out the mess. Paul, who had married into a family of high-powered executive types, was becoming more and more vocal in his complaints about how things were going. The solid Beatle front that had seemed so impervious to outsiders was showing distinct signs of cracks. Paul disappeared to his farm in Scotland to sulk, the Lennons became increasingly involved in the most abstract art and most obvious politics, both at the same time. In the midst of all this strain and discord, there was a movie waiting to be made. This one was to be simpler than the ones that had preceded it, with their elaborate props and costumes and sight gags and different locations. *Let It Be* would show the Beatles, as the Beatles, in their natural habitat, the recording studio. It would bring the audience into a situation where few of them had ever been, giving one the feeling of being an insider at an important event, a Beatle record session. Their friends, the Rolling Stones, still did a lot of touring and filmed the behind-the-scenes action that ended with their tragic concert in Altamont, California, as *Gimme Shelter*. Since touring was gone from the Beatles' schedule, the studio sessions were it.

More than just a movie, more than just a documentary, it was to be the Beatles' last appearance together.

The long and winding road had come to a dead end.

Many different reasons were given for the break-up of the group, none of which mattered very much. It was announced that each of the four, while remaining friends, would now pursue the separate interests that had partially occupied them previously. John and George had each had solo albums before the breakup and Paul and Ringo caught up very quickly with their first efforts, released one month before and one month after the *Let It Be* soundtrack, respectively.

For all the couples except the Lennons, life went on peacefully enough for a while. The Harrisons continued to explore their interests in Eastern matters, the Starrs expanded their family, the McCartneys devoted themselves to each other, slipping into almost semi-retirement for months at a time. Only for John and Yoko did life seem fraught with problems.

Had they too chosen to live quietly, perhaps they would have enjoyed a more hassle-free existence. But they had become very much public people. They came to the United States, and John would sit in at clubs with the performers who were playing. Yoko gave exhibitions of her always controversial artwork. They spoke out on news issues of the day, aligning themselves very strongly with first, the peace movement, and then women's liberation. They put on a show in Toronto where they performed while completely concealed in large bags. Everything they did tended to have shock value. And if the public didn't overreact, the government did, and the two were suddenly faced with deportation.

The government of the United States labeled them undesirable aliens because of a minor hearing which was still pending at the time in England. The Lennons protested explaining that one of their primary reasons for living here was so that Yoko could continue her efforts to locate her child from her former marriage. Thousands of people came to their support and the matter seemed to die. John took up with a new group called Elephant's Memory and worked and recorded with them.

During this time relations between the four former teammates seemed to be amiable enough. They played on each other's records and seemed to imply well, yeah, maybe, we will get back together again someday.

Paul, with wife Linda, leaves court after seeking action that would break up the Beatles' partnership, February 19, 1971. UPI

Ringo and Maureen leave for a Swiss vacation a few weeks
after Paul's move in court. The other Beatles made no
comment on the action, which is still being decided. UPI

But then in February 1971 the bombshell exploded. Accompanied by his wife, Linda, Paul appeared in the High Court in London and asked that the Beatles' entire joint companies be split up completely. Although it had been somewhat expected, it was still a dismal happening. It was an act that seemed final in its implications. People don't usually sue their best friends. Differences within families, which is what the Beatles were, have a way of being smoothed over and worked out.

The others took a somewhat joking attitude about Paul's move, at least publicly. They didn't want to discuss it, really. The one who was most hurt by it all was John, and he, in his characteristic way, made the only outcry. In the fall of '71, after Paul's legal action, John did an album with his Plastic Ono Band called *Imagine*. On it he sang a song that asked "How Do You Sleep?" that is clearly addressed to Paul. It puts down his wife, his in-laws (they were active in the legal matter), and, perhaps bitterest of all, his music. It mentions the oddball hoax that claimed Paul was dead, and says that the people who said it were right. It has a line that goes "the only thing you done was yesterday," and while yesterday doesn't have quotation marks around it, John's meaning is very clear.

Yesterday *was* done.

TODAY

"When I was younger, so much younger than today..."

Ringo has done another album. All three of the other Beatles are on it, but alas, not together. Each new album which George, since the breakup the most prolific Beatle, produces not only surpasses the last, but comes closest to the quality that the four together had achieved. John has Elephant's Memory; Paul was Wings; they both have wives who play or sing on their husbands' records. Paul can take his family to the ballet and not be recognized and John can perform at a giant charity benefit without being mobbed.

And they can all still break up charts anytime they want to! Paul did one of his loveliest ballads since "Yesterday" called "My Love" and it rose to number one as swiftly as any Beatles single would have in the old days. The album that it comes from, *Red Rose Speedway,* was in the number-one long-play spot until it got bumped off by *Living in the Material World* — George's newest! And superseding both new efforts were the two double albums, *Beatles 1962-1966* and *Beatles 1967-1970* containing samplings of the best of all the old output. The cream-of-the-cream of all Beatle music, the two albums sold as if

Beatlemania was still at its height. You could look at the weekly music charts, check the Top Ten, then close your eyes, open your ears, and make believe that nothing *had* changed your world, just as the Beatles had promised in their last release together, "Across the Universe." But the song on the other side of the disc was more accurate. "The Long and Winding Road" was the incredible route the Beatles had taken in their relatively short time together,

Paul appears on his first television special, April 16, 1973. He included oldies like "Yesterday" and the new music he wrote for the film "Live and Let Die," the James Bond epic.
UPI

barely a decade from their scruffy beginnings as a sometime band to the unprecedented pinnacle of the world's most popular group. They had changed us in so many ways — how we talked, how we listened, the clothes we wore, the way we wore our hair, how we danced and thought and sang. If the way we still buy their albums is any indication, that long and winding road the Beatles took still leads them to our door.

Paul shows up at the London premiere of "Live and Let Die" in tuxedo and bow tie, but without a shirt. Luckily, the Beatles aren't as influential in setting new styles as they once were! UPI

What the Beatles accomplished stands as a legacy for everyone, but most especially for young people. Before the whole world went Beatle-crazy, the group and their followers were scoffed at, scorned, and rebuked by the older generation. Their music was characterized as noise and senseless screaming by people who didn't bother to listen. They were held responsible for everything that was wrong with the world, from the new dances to crime in the streets. To young people, the Beatles represented everything that was *right* with the world — music and love and hope and peace. Young people saw very little that they liked in the world their parents' generation had created. But the world of the Beatles was something else, full of sunshine and young ideas. It took their dreams of love and made them real. This new music freed the mind as well as the body from the overstructured rules of the dos and don'ts. It also created a bond between fans and followers. Whether you shouted at a concert or shared listening to a new record, you were one with the people around you. It was a shelter from the outside world, where people were complaining about alienation and loneliness and lack of communication. When you were listening to the Beatles, those feelings were absent. Everyone was communicating and the message was a warm one. So perhaps it was jealousy of what young people had found that turned the older generation off. Or maybe it was the realization that the youngsters they found it impossible to get through to were being reached very easily by four young men with a brand new style. So much time has passed since the Beatles became acceptable, it is hard to remember the days when they were being denounced in round ringing terms.

Even when the Beatles were at their peak, the question was, who will be next? Can anyone else ever be that big again? Can another group come along who will mean as much as the Beatles did? Probably not. There will be new favorites, of course, but that they will achieve the eminence of the Beatles is highly unlikely.

John Lennon, the man who almost single-handedly started the long hair trend, sports a close-shaven look at the Watergate hearings, which he attended with Yoko. UPI

Their current positions do a lot to explain why this is so. If the Beatles had continued to capture public favor, if they had continued to grow and lead their fans as they had been doing, they might have, in their declining years, paved the way for the next great take-over. But their splitting up served to destroy the world they had created. We gave our everything, is their fans' unconscious reaction, all our love, all our loyalty, our total devotion. In turn, they should have given us at least a few more years of themselves, their ideas, the security of their just being there, a solid edifice in the ever-crumbling world. They were our warm blanket that magically adjusted itself to our new size and our new needs. They were also our magic carpet that took us wherever we wanted to go and wherever they wanted to take us: Usually the two destinations were the same — that was their real magic! Nobody ripped that blanket/carpet apart. They did it themselves. It didn't get older, just got better. We didn't desert them — they deserted us. And that's why we'll probably never let anyone do it to us like that again.

Nobody knows exactly where the Beatles stand today. Not even themselves. It's shrouded in mystery, legal, personal, what have you. It's all confusion, uncertainty, big business, financial angles, noncommunication. John won't talk to Paul. Or is it that Paul won't talk to John? Whatever it is, it isn't Beatledom. It's the outside world that they themselves distrusted and gave us an alternative to. Now they're part of it. That's what hurts.

The Beatles can't communicate?
Is that possible?
What does that have to do with music?
What does it have to do with *us*?

Ringo is still bushy and fully bearded as well, as he and Maureen leave London for Budapest and Elizabeth Taylor's birthday party. UPI

Is it any wonder that sometimes we don't even care what happens?

Sometimes when we listen to the music, we find ourselves wondering still: Will Sgt. Pepper's Yellow Submarine Magical Mystery Tour ever run again?

Yesterday ... and Today, now, what about Tomorrow?

TOMORROW

"One day you'll look to see I've gone,
For tomorrow may rain so I'll follow the sun."

Exactly where that sun will be shining is a little difficult to chart at present. If there were still four corners to the world, we might someday find a Beatle sitting in each of them. Paul could be hiding on his farm in Aberdeen, Scotland. George would be in India, studying and meditating. John could be in New York, writing letters to newspapers and playing guitar for the fun of it, in clubs that haven't been able to afford him since 1963. Ringo could be a big movie star in Hollywood or visiting Elizabeth Taylor on her yacht.

But the world has no corners — it isn't square. It's round. "Because the world is round it turns me on," they wrote. What it turns the Beatles on to is still music. They will be writing it and performing it wherever they may be. The big question remains: Will they ever be doing it together, all four, the way it used to be?

Paul has Wings, but can they soar as high as he used to? They are all good musicians, hand-picked by Paul himself after many, many tries — Denny Seiwell, Denny Laine, Henry McCullough — but they're far from being the Beatles.

PAUL

GEORGE

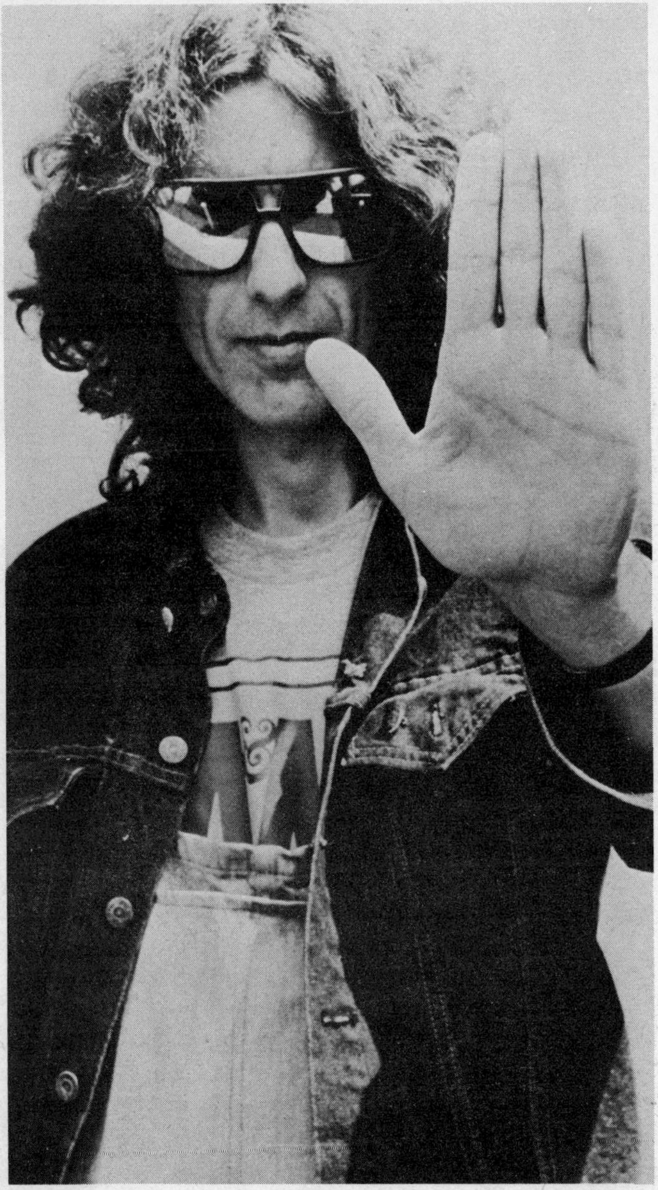

John has Elephant's Memory, but he recalls only too clearly the days of *Sgt. Pepper,* as he reminds Paul on that "How Do You Sleep?" lyric. It is a fine back-up band — Stan Bronstein, Richard Frank, Gary Van Scyoc, Adam Ippolito, Tex Gabriel, and sometimes others sitting in — a good New York rock band, but they aren't the Beatles, either.

"I didn't leave the Beatles; the Beatles left the Beatles," Paul has said in his own defense. Whether or not that's true, it does point up the fact that the only thing that separates the Beatles is themselves. If they really wanted to get together again, they

could. In fact, getting together would probably be a lot simpler than separating is proving to be. Pitch out the lawyers and bring back the sound technicians, the re-mixers, the arrangers, and producers, the back-up musicians, and the vocalists. Write new songs and use new instruments and explore new ideas. Mix John's politics and Paul's romanticism and George's philosophy and Ringo's Ringoism (he still can't play a drum roll, but who cares?) and throw a giant party for the whole world! *Do* it, Beatles!

We love you, yeah yeah yeah....

And, lest we forget, back in the beginning . . . UPI

A PERSONAL NOTE FROM THE AUTHOR

I was there at the beginning. At JFK Airport when they first landed. The very first press conference at the Airport. The rehearsals and the live performance for the Sullivan show. The press conference and reception at the Plaza Hotel. The first concert, onstage, at Carnegie Hall.   Later, Forest Hills. Shea Stadium. The press conference to announce the formation of Apple. Three screenings of the unfinished *Yellow Submarine* (one without sound!). Talking, touching, autographs, mementos, memories. Yes, I was there at the beginning. And in the middle.

I don't want to be there at the end.